THE SEASONS IN MR. GREEN'S GARDEN

IT'S AUTUMN

by Ruth Owen

Ruby Tuesday Books

Published in 2024 by Ruby Tuesday Books Ltd.

Editor: Mark J. Sachner
Design: Tammy West
Production: John Lingham

Photo credits:
Alamy: 13BL (Michelle Howell), 18T (Malcolm Schuyl), 19T (Michael Grant Wildlife); Dwight Kuhn: 18B; Nature Picture Library: 12L (Duncan Usher), 19B (Alan Williams), 21T (Stephen Dalton; Shutterstock: Cover (Karel Gallas/LilKar/Danita Delimont), 5 (Jungle Bandana/Bonnie Taylor Barry/perlphoto/Sander Meertins Photography), 6 (Maria Evseyeva), 8 (Jana Danek jdm.foto/AntMak), 9 (CLS Digital Arts/BBA Photography), 10B (A Dragan), 12R (Cones/Lois GoBe), 15 (photka/Kazakov Maksim/Tom Pavlasek/Art Cook Studio), 16 (Artush/Ryan Green Photography/Cornel Constantin), 17 (ab Images/Ammak/Ermak Oksana/Lilkar/Lonny Garris), 20 (Jennifer Bosvert/Gregory Johnston).

Library of Congress Control Number: 2023952430

Print (Hardback) ISBN 978-1-78856-377-2
Print (Paperback) ISBN 978-1-78856-378-9
ePub ISBN 978-1-78856-380-2

Published in Minneapolis, MN
Printed in the United States

www.rubytuesdaybooks.com

Contents

In a garden, there is always
something to look forward to. . . .

Welcome to the Garden

This is Mr. Green and his friend and neighbor, Mo.

There was a messy, trash-filled place in the city where they live.

So they cleaned it up and grew a beautiful community garden for everyone to enjoy.

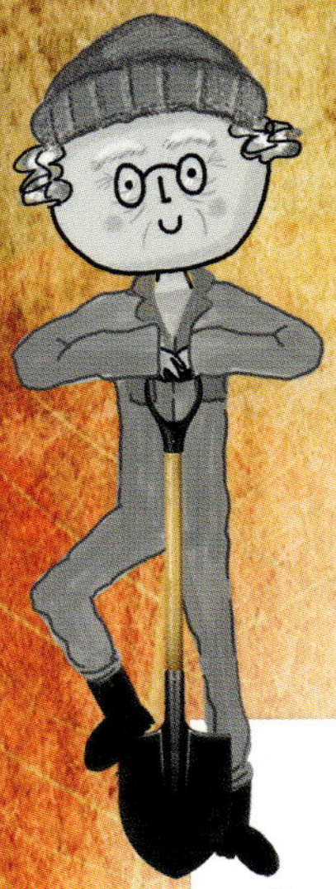

Mr. Green says:

A garden is a very good place to learn about the seasons, and watch them change.

Every year there are **4** seasons.

Each one lasts for about three months.

Autumn...

September October November

Winter...

December January February

Spring...

March April May

Summer...

June July August

Mo says:

Let's discover what happens in the garden in autumn!

How Do We Know It's Autumn?

As summer comes to an end and autumn begins, the weather gets cooler.

It may be sunny in the daytime, but cold at night.

Sometimes, the weather in autumn is **foggy**, windy, and there may be storms.

Each day during autumn, there is a little less daytime and more nighttime.

A day is 24 hours long. Daytime begins when the Sun rises and ends when it sets. When the Sun is not in the sky, it is dark and nighttime.

Through the spring and summer, pumpkin plants have been growing.

Now, the pumpkins are ready to **harvest**—just in time for Halloween!

It's Acorn Time!

All summer, acorns have been growing on the oak tree.

Now they are brown and ready to fall to the ground.

The acorns settle in the soil and **rotting** leaves.

Inside each acorn is a **seed** that may grow into a new oak tree.

The squirrels that live in the garden are busy collecting and burying acorns.

In winter, when there is less food around, they will dig up and eat their buried acorns.

Mr. Green says:

A squirrel doesn't find all the food it buries.

Some acorns will stay in the soil and start to grow.

Why Is the Oak Tree Changing Color?

A tree makes food for energy in its leaves.

It does this with water, **carbon dioxide** gas from the air, and sunlight.

The leaves capture sunlight using green stuff called chlorophyll.

Mr. Green says:

When autumn comes, the oak tree gets ready to have a winter rest.

It stops making food and removes the green chlorophyll from its leaves.

Now, it's possible to see the other colors of the leaves.

An Oak Tree Leaf Changing Color

Finally, one by one, the leaves die and drop to the ground.
Tree roots
The fallen leaves are food for millipedes, woodlice, slugs, snails, and worms.

Autumn Is a Time for Seeds

In summer, the garden was filled with colorful flowers. Now the flowers are dying and producing seeds.

The seeds drop onto the soil or blow on the breeze to new growing places.

Next spring, each tiny seed could become a new plant.

The seeds are an energy-packed food for the garden's birds.

All summer, fruit has been growing on the garden's apple trees.

Now the apples are **ripe** and ready to harvest.

Some apples fall to the ground and become food for birds, mice, snails, slugs, and other animals.

Inside each apple that falls to the ground are seeds that may grow into new apple trees.

There's Lots to Do in the Garden

As summer comes to an end, there are fruits and vegetables to harvest.

Mo's BIG Garden Harvest

Plant and grass clippings, dead leaves, and vegetable peelings have been rotting on the **compost heap**.

Now they have turned to crumbly new soil that we put on the garden.

Next spring, all the good stuff in the compost will help feed the plants.

In autumn, we plant daffodils, tulips, and other **bulbs** in the ground and in flowerpots.

The bulbs will wait in the soil all winter. In spring, they will grow colorful flowers.

Mr. Green says:

We collect seeds from the garden to plant in spring. But we leave plenty for our bird friends to eat!

How Do We Help Our Wildlife Friends?

When autumn comes, we help the garden animals get ready for winter.

Bird table

We set up bird tables where we can give the birds extra food.

We build bug hotels from logs, scraps of timber, bark, bamboo canes, bricks, and other materials.

Small animals such as bees, lacewings, ladybugs, spiders, centipedes, and woodlice will shelter here in winter.

Spider

Woodlouse

Ladybug

Centipede

We make heaps of rocks, logs, twigs, and autumn leaves.

These places are good winter homes for toads, frogs, snails, and **minibeasts**.

Logs

Rocks

Autumn leaves

Twigs

Compost heap

Toad

Mo says:

We leave some compost in the compost heap.

It will become a warm winter hiding place for toads, **insects**, slugs, and other animals.

See You in Spring, Bumblebees!

Under the grass in the garden, there is a bumblebee nest.

Inside the nest, a queen bee has been laying eggs. Fat **larvae** hatch from the eggs.

The larvae become female worker bees that gather **nectar** and **pollen** from flowers. This food is shared by the queen, workers, and larvae.

In late summer, some of the larvae that hatch are new queen bees. Others are male bees.

The young queens and males leave their home to mate with bees from other nests.

Each new, young queen eats lots of nectar to build up her body fat. Then she finds a place to hibernate.

As autumn comes, the old queen and her worker bees die.

In spring, each new queen bee will lay eggs and start her own nest of worker bees.

Autumn Will Soon Be Over

In autumn, some of the garden trees and bushes produce berries. Inside each berry are tiny seeds.

When birds eat juicy berries, the seeds go through their **digestive system**. Then the birds poop out the seeds in new growing places!

Robin chicks that hatched in spring or summer are nearly grown-up.

Next year, they will be ready to have chicks of their own.

As the weather gets cooler, a caterpillar attaches itself to the garden shed with silk.

It wriggles out of its skin and becomes a **pupa**.

The pupa will stay this way until spring, when it will change into a butterfly.

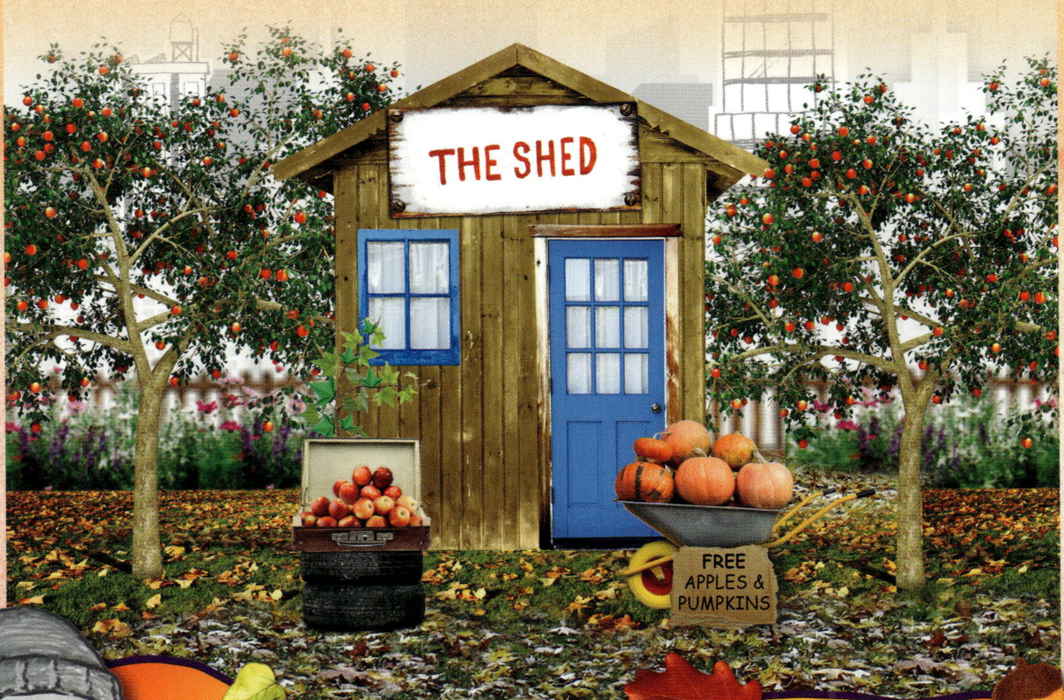

Mr. Green says:

As autumn comes to an end, the garden is ready to take a long rest. Soon it will be winter. But that's a whole other book. . . .

Mr. Green's Garden Glossary

bulb
A round underground part that some plants grow from. Food for the new plant is stored in the bulb.

carbon dioxide
A colorless gas in the air that plants use to make food.

compost heap
A large pile or box of plant clippings, vegetable peelings, and other material that rots and becomes new soil.

digestive system
The stomach, intestines, and other body parts of a person or animal that digest food and make poop.

foggy
A type of weather when clouds of tiny water drops form close to the ground and make it difficult to see around you.

harvest
To pick, cut down, or dig up vegetables and fruits when they are ready to eat.

hibernate
To spend the winter in a deep sleep without eating or drinking.

insect
A tiny animal with six legs and a body in three main parts. Most insects have wings.

larva
A young insect that hatches from an egg. A caterpillar is a type of larva.

mate
To come together to produce young.

minibeast
A small animal such as an insect, spider, slug, or worm.

nectar
A sweet liquid made by flowers.

pollen
A colored dust that is made by flowers, and is needed for making seeds.

pupa
One of the stages in the life cycle of some insects. For example, the four stages in a butterfly's life cycle are egg, caterpillar, pupa, and adult butterfly.

ripe
Fully grown and ready to be picked or eaten.

rotting
Decomposing, or breaking down.

season
One of the four parts of a year. The seasons are winter, spring, summer, and autumn.

seed
A tiny part of a plant that contains all the material needed to grow a new plant.

Index

If you enjoyed this book, discover the story of how Mr. Green and his friend Mo created their wonderful garden.

Hardback: 978-1-78856-195-2
eBook: 978-1-78856-237-9